Evolution
Collection of poems and short notes

Evolution
Collection of poems and short notes

APARNA GURU

BLACK EAGLE BOOKS
Dublin, USA | Bhubaneswar, India

Black Eagle Books
USA address:
7464 Wisdom Lane
Dublin, OH 43016

India address:
E/312, Trident Galaxy, Kalinga Nagar,
Bhubaneswar-751003, Odisha, India

E-mail: info@blackeaglebooks.org
Website: www.blackeaglebooks.org

First International Edition Published by
Black Eagle Books, 2023

EVOLUTION
by **Aparna Guru**

Copyright © Aparna Guru

All rights reserved. No part of this publication may be reproduced, stored in a retrieval system, or transmitted, in any form or by any means, electronic, mechanical, photocopying, recording or otherwise without the prior permission of the publisher.

Cover and inner art : Aparna Guru
Interior Design: Ezy's Publication

ISBN- 978-1-64560-403-7 (Paperback)
Library of Congress Control Number: 2023940282

Printed in the United States of America

Life is easy...Life is difficult
And experiences don't last forever

But something significant leaves its marks
On the sands of time
Life moves on
But something stays behind

Something...
That prepares us for our evolution

Dedicated to life that creates the possibility
to live, love and learn

A gift to Millie nani, the most affectionate sister I have.

Contents

CREATION

Evolution	13
Autogenous	15
Big bang	17

LOVE

Yesterday	21
Waiting	23
I'll be back	26
Face of love	27
Wounded stars	29
Answers	31
With you	33

DEVOTION

Face to face	37
Devotion	39
Gratitude	41
Pride	43
Seeker	45
Prayer	46
Faith	48

QUEST

Heart significant	53
Life and death	54
Movement	56
Let it go	58
Words	59
Solitude	60

WINTER

Charm	63
Friends	65
Snowy winter	67

NOTES

Dawn till dusk	71
Puddle	72
Sunset	73
Autumn moon	74
Soulmate	75
Living room	76

Creation

Evolution

In the beginning...
If there was any
It was just a dot.
No size...No shape
Plain full stop.

Perhaps from that end
A new origin emerged...
Gently gliding down
The time's curve...

To find itself again
With long forgotten forms...
To lose itself again
In the arms of love...

To wear again
The garments of life & death
The colors of sorrow & joy...

To see itself through
The truth's clear rays...

To grow again
Amidst little things...
Nothing insignificant...None out of line

And to rise beyond
The perfection's static stature
Sometimes still...Sometimes in motion

A rock now...An eagle later
Or just a plain dot.

Autogenous

Is poetry just a skill of the brain
Or a song of the heart...
Is it purity of thoughts
Or simply a game of words?

Why there is poetry
And why it couldn't be
Just another sentence...
Following all the rules of grammar
Lucid...Straight

Poetry feels otherwise...
Ah! How hard that's to explain
No mere sentence could suffice...

Perhaps a bird can
Hopping from branch to branch
Flowers to flowers
With its beautiful plumage...
Shining with myriad of colors
Spreading the vibes of joy...

But as I try to step in
To get a closer glimpse
To clasp this moment of bliss
To the far it flies away...

Sometimes in my lonely hours
When outside & still...
A small beautiful bird
Finds its way to me...
Delighting my heart
Breaking my monotony...

Poetry is as such...Perhaps
Reveals itself...
In its own moment...In its own ways

Hard to say...
If it is me, who creates the poetry
Or the poetry creates itself...

Big Bang

Once upon a time…
The clocks didn't have any hands
No machinery was there to measure
Hours…Minutes…Seconds

And in that ancient era…
Someone said
There was
No earth…No stars…No nebulas

How things could have been
In a time beyond time
In a space without space…

What was held into what
What gave things birth?
I chose to call it the heart…

And heart…You know
Like the river flows
With a strong will
To meet the sea…

And heart...You know
Like the northern lake
Complete...Content
Still...Silent

So, from that stillness
Mystics call it,
Nirvana...Nothingness
Arises a little desire to be loved...

And love...You know
Nothing less than an explosion
Scientists call it Big Bang...

Love

Yesterday

Love again...
In the empty afternoon moments
Urging me to converse
Caressing with its sweet touch

As memories in my mind
Heart's delight
As new dreams waiting to be woven
Along the time's thread...

Until I meet you again
Days...Months...Ages
Would you still look back
When you hear my voice...

Would you care
To stop by...To feel
My closeness...My silence

Would you wait there
By the glass door...
Until my seeking glance
Meets yours...

Would you call again & ask
While you still doubt
I might not care to answer...

Would you love me
As you did...As you do
Now...And forever
Without a vow...

Would you love me
For the sake of yourself...
And not for me

I'll be with you
In case you need a hand
A smile...When you're distressed
A poetry...To stir your heart
A friend...To hear your words

Look again...
I'm closer than yesterday

Waiting

By the golden fire
I sat one evening
And searched for your shadow
By my side...

The crackling flames
Broke my sweet slumber
Spent on the memory lane
We walked together...

You...With your quick, restless steps
Me...Trying hard to match
Completely lost in your presence
In your words...
While all the seasons passed by
Unnoticed...Unheard

Checked...If I had missed your call
Though I knew...It was just a false hope

After a moment...
Stood close to the window
Watching the passing silhouettes
In the faint evening light...
Imagining your shape

If it was you...
Wearing your black winter jacket

The blue bird...
That suddenly appeared from nowhere
Fluttering behind the cherry shrub
Had it come to signal your arrival?

Went through the old pages of my book
And laughed again at the absurd sketch you drew
Reliving the very first moment
We created something together...

Feeling your warm touch
As my hands touched those strokes...
Feeling the nearness of your soul
As I read the words you wrote...

Scribbled your name
On my notebook again...

In my desolate moments
Amidst the empty desks...
Along the empty lanes
Your voice in me gets louder...
As if trying to tell me
I'm close...I'm near

Dipped in the deep colors of love
Smiles...Tears
Happy...Hopeful
But, never without you...

Alarmed at the approaching footsteps...

I opened the door of my heart
And my waiting began...

I'll be back

Wait a moment
I'll be back in a jiffy
Sun or rain
You'll find me again...

So, don't despair
I'm always in your heart...

I'll follow
Wherever you go
I'm the shadow of your soul...

And keep that light of love burning...

We are the travelers of the time
Sometimes near...Sometimes far
But, never apart...
Finding each other
When calls the heart...

Face of love

The face of love...
Hiding behind
The mask of right and wrong...

Reasons...
Too fragile
Shattered by the slightest
Touch of truth

As truth...
Permeates through
Those obscured layers of vanity

Pretense...Pride
Rules...Risks of society

To unravel the unseen
To unbound something
That was never in chains...

Love lives in the
Realms beyond reasons...

And along those
Prohibited lanes...

No longer bound by
Fear...Pain

Lovers find their ways
To each other...

Crossing over the
Thousand tides...
In the whirlpool of
Death...Life

To meet...To be met
Love...Unveiled

Wounded stars

Things falling down...

Are these dead things
Falling from the space
When they could
Carry themselves no longer...

Or the lonely hearts
Beating far
Heading home
To find love...

Or may be broken stars
With wounded hearts
Crushed into pieces
By the blow of betrayal...

But who can betray the stars
Do they have lovers too
Do they feel lost like us?

Then, they will find their way
Just like we do...

In another space
In another time...

The broken pieces will assemble
A new masterpiece will be made
A new star will born
A new life will begin...

And it will be all light again...
Brighter than before

Falling...
A rough start
For a better beginning...

Answers

Thoughts...Dilemmas
Questions...Answers

So many things...
Reel up in my mind...

Answers...I want to hear
Answers...I escape from
Answers...I can never conjure

I'm afraid...I'm in love
In love...I'm tangled

Body and Soul
Heart and Mind

Not sure...
Think...I've disappeared
To a land
With landscapes blurred...

Does love need clarity?

Perhaps not
Or it would be just ordinary

Bound by necessities...

Love knows what it feels
Love is always complete.

What if...
Lovers never express themselves

Not a word about love
No kisses...Not holding on to each other

Would their love persist...
Can love survive without a promise?

Love is an expression in itself
Love will find a thousand ways.

No Clarity...Commitments...Calculations
A heart in love is guided by
Faith alone...

With you

Is it you...Knocking softly
At the door of my heart...
I can feel the music again
But there is a faint despair...

Ask me not next time
If you could come in...
Don't remember a moment
When you are not within...

Ask me not...If I love you
Look into my eyes...Find the truth

Don't know...Love leads us where
I believe...
It is strong enough to change the world...
I'm afraid though
Hold me tight in your arms...

True...Fair...Unfair
Faith...Doubt
Love is a ride
On an uncertain route...

And yet worth living for
And to die...
Without love
Nothing makes sense...

Devotion

Face to Face

Let's connect
Alive in this moment
We're close
We're together...

Don't do another thing
No distraction please...
I'm waiting to be felt
I'm waiting to be seen...

So, touch me with your heart
See me through your soul...
I want to know you
I need to be known...

Keep your mind unmoved
Let me dive into your depths...
Only still water can
Clearly reflect a face...

Remove your veils of vanity
Pride...Possessions...Pretense
All that is false
All that fades...

And let me find you there
In the realms beyond despair
In a moment beyond time
When all feels divine...

I see you...You see me!

Devotion

As the sun shines in a winter dawn
Warm smoke rises from the lotus pond

Fresh morning air...Mixed with mist
Drops of water on the green leaves...

Like tiny silver pearls...

Flowers blooming with beauty
Sweet fragrance
White Jasmines are ready to be plucked...

So are the red Mandaras...Marigolds

To adorn the feet of my Lord
To decorate his divine chamber...

Birds have left their nests since long
I can hear only the sacred songs...

Copper bells ringing...
Holy chants...Hymns

The humming of the flower seller
As she threads in the pink lotus...

And the silence of the old monk
Meditating in a desolate corner...
Counting the beads of holy basils
Bound to his fragile fingers...

In the river by the shrine
Little boats set sail
With the offerings to the divine...

Flowers...Leaves
Incense...Sweets
Earthen lamps...Glowing bright

Floating on the dancing waves...
Tiny vessels of colors & lights
Hopes...Wishes

A march of moving stars
On the water...
Far into the bluish mist
Blurred...Disappeared

Gratitude

Never said…I did it all
I succeeded for
Some unknown cause
And also for the known
But never did it all alone…

If I win…Who should take the credit
If I lose…Who should take the blame
Who should I thank
For this drop of knowledge
In my brain…

This spark of fire
You've placed in my heart
This seed of growth
You've planted in my soul
How could I best express to you
My gratitude…My love

Like the sun to the flowers
Moon to the sea
I'm drawn to your presence
Filling me within…

Every step…I take
Is a winning step
Doesn't matter
If I fall…If I fail

When I fall
You give me the strength to rise…
When I fail
You guide me as the stars in the night…

What was there to gain
What is there to lose
Everything I have
All comes from you…
Everything I do
I give it to you…

God…You contain me
In your warm & sublime heart

God…I contain you
In my laughter
In my darkest hours…

Pride

Pride...
Not sure...What should I be proud of

I'll start from the best in the list
Loved ones are the greatest gift...

And love is not my making...
If I'm the earth...Love is the seed

Planted by some blessed hands
Where's my pride in that?
Just a great sense of gratitude
Immeasurable...

Then comes the mind...

If I'm good...I'm all comfortable
If I'm bad...I'm in doubt

And mind is not my making...
If I'm the canvas...Mind is the art

Sometimes happy...Sometimes sad
Or an abstract...

Drawn by some blessed hands
Where's my pride in that?
Just a great sense of wonder
Ceaseless...

Body comes next
Brain, limbs and senses...

And body is not my making...
If I'm a chariot...Body is my wheels

Partly pulled by heart
Partly pulled by mind
Following the nature's guide...

Written by some blessed hands
Where's my pride in that?
Just a great sense of faith
Unfailing...Ageless

Seeker

I know...I'm seeking hard
Deep within my passionate heart
Your reflection...

I looked for you
Whenever you called...
In the moments of loneliness
In the moments of chaos...

I feel you
When I enter your sacred shrine
In my silent hours
Contemplating the beauty of the worlds...

But I find you closer
In my happiest moments
With love by my side...
As that's the only time
I give myself to you completely...

You are...
A friend...A healer
My muse...My master

Prayer

Dear God
Protector of all realms...
Protect me from evil
Protect me from ignorance...

Protect me from sickness
Protect me from sin
Stronger may I live...

Dear God
Kind & full of love
Be always by my side
Day or night...

As a friend,
A teacher...A guide

Be always in my heart...
May my aspirations be pure
Driving me to the right path...

Dear God
Eternal & true
Mighty...Merciful

May I be steady & wise
Firm in my resolve...
May I rise again & always
Success or failure...

Bless me with your light
Bless me with your love...

Bless us with your light
Bless us with your love...

Faith

I'm an empty vessel, God
Carrying only your force...

Floating on the sea of thousand tides
High and Low...
Propelled by some unseen hands
To a faraway land unknown...

Often in my troubled times
While waving my way
Through the storms...

The high frightening tides
Roaring thunders
Ragged edges of the rocks...

My sail is broken
So is my boat...
And what makes me steer ahead
If not the spirit's force...

I keep on sailing
And the storm is gone...

Often in my happier times
On the calm waters
Serene...Endless

Under the watch of night stars
Guiding me ahead...

I witness the colors of beauty
Feel the rainbow of joy...

And live a moment of love
Eternal...Pure

When all doubts fade away
When all fears gone...

Quest

Heart significant

Lotus heart...Seat of love
All aspirations rise from you
In you they submerge...

Driven by the desires
Are the thoughts...And the deeds
Mind pursues
What the heart conceives...

And what's destiny
Good...Bad
If it's not an idea
Escaped the mind
Checked...Unchecked

And memory couldn't track its source
Named it as mysterious force...

So, what greater than the heart
Sublime...Sane
Steering the intuitive mind's path
On the life's occult plane...

Life and Death

Find me the colors
Want to paint a face...
That depicts life
Unveils death...

Red...Yellow...Blue
Myriad of hues
Mixed with care
Millions of forms appear...

For the cold death
Found no colors for that...

If life is poetry
Death is a deeper mystery...

Life...
Beating of the hearts
Blooming of flowers
And everything that shines...

All ardent...All alive

Death...
Lost or Found
Died or Healed
Aged or Renewed

Still...Spotless

Life brings answers
Death...Speechless

Movement

Movement...
Stirs the still mind
My gaze following
The autumn wind

Carrying the fallen leaves far...

Red...Yellow...Gold
Colors of despair and hope

All lost or found at last
All free or still bound by hearts...

Falling...Floating...Still
Waiting for another thought to begin

To bloom...To move

The brook by the hill side...

Sweet babbling of the ripples
Water running over round rocks...

Up & down
Swirling around...

Playing a new tune...

Each time it touches
The drooping branches
Swaying in the wind...

Tiny twigs & leaves
Start their sail
To another shore
Murmuring a fresh tone...

The mysterious music of the flowing stream,
Rocks...Twigs...Fallen leaves
Washing away
All my woes...All my worries

Lost in the beauty of movement & flow
Peace and stillness follow...

Let it go

Highs...Lows
Hope...Despair
Faith...Doubt
All opposites appear
In the roller-coaster ride of life
On one thread of time...

As I struggle to find a way out of
The unchosen ones
In my illuding moments of bliss
All moments fade
Good or bad
Before my eyes...

There is something still
True...Timeless
Always by my side...
Asking me not to bind a thing
Asking me to set myself free...

Words

From the thoughts to the words
And back to the thoughts...
Waves washing the shore
And then withdraw...
On the wet sand...My feet sink low
Asked the words...What's your goal

The sea brings the tides back
This time with greater strength
Wind blows hard
But I could hear no answers...

So, just stood still
Contemplating the beauty of the sea
Waves moving back and forth
Setting sun...A flock of gulls

And the blue lonely boat
Sailing far...
Far from the words
Into the emerald vast...

Into the sublime silence...

Solitude

Life takes mysterious turns...
Oblivious to the truth
I run after my daily chores
My emotions...

Picking myself up after each fall...
Flying to cloud nine
Each time I conquer...

But, in the long lonely hours
When I've nothing else to do
None to care...No dreams to pursue
Through the empty spaces of my mind
My soul tries to peep through...

And my heart rushes forth to receive
A glance of the truth...

Where, all questions answered...
All seeking ends...
Just to check,
If everything makes sense...
All fine...All fair?

Solitude opens the gate
To the greater knowledge...

Winter

Charm

Tonight's air has something strange in it
Never before I've felt like this...

My mind is as clear as the empty lanes
Tireless traveling oblivious to its end...

My heart feels like the enormous heaven
Embracing all I've felt, all I've met
All precious...All makes sense

Night brings solace
Nullifies all desires...

In a day, there are things to conquer
At night, I simply surrender...

Countless moments pass
As I fall into the night's arms...

As I look through my glass window...
Tall tress...Quieter they feel
As the winter wind passes through
The empty branches of Birch...

With no leaves to rustle
No creatures to scare...
Steady as the meditating monks
Standing unmoved...Calm

Horizon lined with pines clad in snow
Sky filled with bright light
Some new colors...

That neither belong to the day
Nor to the night...

Painting the white fields of snow
Emerald...Pink...Gold

And the tiny town lamps
Glowing far...
Bright & blurred
Like the evening stars...

I stand still
As the night passes through my eyes...
Letting it conquer my mind
Losing all sense of time...

Until I find myself again...
Out of night's charm
Beyond this mystic moment...

Friends

There is someone watching you...
Through the other side
Of your window...

Quietly...
He observes all your moves
Your secret dancing in the kitchen
Like a swan...
Sometimes like a fish...
Sometimes like the earth itself
With all that tireless twirling...

And watch again
Hot tea overflows
Stains on your stove...

You've got other friends there
With whom you catch up
During your cooking interval...

As the porridge simmers
Potatoes waiting to be softer...

A line of pine trees
At the end of that intersecting street...

With orange tint crowning their top
During the sunset hours...
Makes the winter feel warm for a while...

The black magpie on the Birch top
So confident...So content
Even the wind would not like to disturb...

And the tiny yellow birds
Confused...Lost
Finding no place to hide in the cold

Searching for a bird house
Perhaps your wooden terrace
Where you often find them
Fluttering by your sofa...

Snowy winter

Winter...
Flakes on the windows
Like tiny quills in silver...

Roofs filled with snow...
Smoke from the red chimney
Slowly rising up...

Rustling pine needles
Little squirrels
Scurrying...Stopping
As the snow slips down
Trembling the leaves...

Fluttering birds
Behind the bushes
By the frozen stream...

I can hear their songs
Or is it a secret conversation
But can't see them still...

Perhaps by the cottony shrubs
Empty branches with snowballs
In that yellow bird box

Cozying up somewhere
But not very far...

Tress filled with snow
Turning into brilliant sculptures
Some familiar...
Some unfathomable shapes...
May be a bear...May be an elf

All carved with care
By some unknown hands...

Leaving the mind to wonder
Beauty of the snowy winter...

Notes

Dawn till dusk

A dawn beautiful...
Silver mist rising from the pool
Filled with white and pink lotus

I could find only one in Blue
Blooming by my side...

Rain on the green hills
Water cascading down as streams...

Somewhere a bit far
On a narrow clear river
Group of white swans float softly...

Flock of birds in the dusk
A swift shadow
Moving over the sunset colors...
Red and Grey
A bit of Orange...

Puddle

Rain has stopped for a while
Grey clouds still fill up the sky
Water dripping from the thatched roof
The little pool of mud
With circles of waves
Waiting to be still...

Sunset

Won't forget that sunset ever
A strange light painted everything gold
Leaving my book on the window shelf
I went straight outdoors...

And found all gleaming
Sky...Houses...Streets

Group of ladies & their joyful talk
Kids playing
Filling the air with dust...

There was noise...There was peace

Autumn moon

Autumn moon...
Rising behind the passing clouds

Making the dark lanes brighter...
Striped with the shadows
Of Eucalyptus...
On the fallen leaves
A shine of silver...

Following my footsteps
Wherever I go...

Soulmate

You are the mirror
Through which I look at myself...

To be known
Is to be with you...

Living room

That empty room of yours
In the evening time...
No furnitures...Feeble light

Walls without
Decoration...Drawings
Windows without
Curtains...Blinds

With uninterrupted view of the sky...

No sofa...No bed
Just the red carpet

And a small blue chair
Where you have kept
Tiny Christmas lights in a jar...

And watch their colored reflections
On the Grey walls...

Pile of books kept in a corner
An open diary
With a half-written poem...

Waiting for the thoughts to return...

∎

Black Eagle Books

www.blackeaglebooks.org
info@blackeaglebooks.org

Black Eagle Books, an independent publisher, was founded as a nonprofit organization in April, 2019. It is our mission to connect and engage the Indian diaspora and the world at large with the best of works of world literature published on a collaborative platform, with special emphasis on foregrounding Contemporary Classics and New Writing.

www.ingramcontent.com/pod-product-compliance
Lightning Source LLC
Chambersburg PA
CBHW020547080526
44583CB00013B/1032